A Short
to th

Best Walks
in Pembrokeshire

by
Tony Roberts

**Sketch Maps and Illustrations
by Elizabeth Roberts**

Abercastle Publications

Enjoy Walking in Pembrokeshire

Most of us have only a limited time for walking, so it seemed a good idea to select some outstanding areas in a countryside where the scenery changes so widely.

I have tried to keep a balance between north and south, between the coast and inland and between long and short walks.

Some walks have had to be left out because of poor parking, or because the Army is in the way, or because of inadequate footpaths. There is as little walking on roads as possible.

While some outstanding long walks require two cars, one at each end to allow more than one person to do the walk without walking back, I have put in as many short walks as possible, so that the whole family can spend an hour or less, rather than face a day's trek.

A word of warning: some parts of the Coast Path are dangerous, and small children should be carefully watched everywhere. Warning notices are totally inadequate so don't expect them. And do wear good shoes or boots; gorse and nettles can be painful.

Footpaths are shown by dotted lines, but I have not shown all public rights of way. I have tried to keep a balance to give walks which are interesting for views and wildlife and also have some historical importance.

Since the book was first written, the Statutory Authority, in most cases the National Park Authority, has greatly improved the footpaths and other amenities, and it is not their fault that the law does not require that all footpaths be way-marked, so you can frequently find a roadside signpost but get lost in the first field. In this booklet we have tried not to use paths where this happens.

The scale of the rough sketch maps is about 2½" to the mile, except for the Preselies which is reduced by about half, and Pembroke town.

Read each walk to see how short walks can be made out of one longer one. And to see which are suitable as round walks by using intermediate footpaths.

The Dyfed Wildlife Trust is abbreviated to its initials, D.W.T. A few useful addresses are given inside the cover.

Contents

Types of Walk

Roughly classified, pages 4, 5, 6, 7, 13, 14, 15, 16, 17, 18, 19, 20, 21, 22, 23, 25, 26, 27, 28 and 29 are coastal walks.

Pages 8, 9, 10, 11, 12 and 32 are hill walks.

Pages 30 and 31 are woodland, and pages 13, 19 and 24 are town walks too.

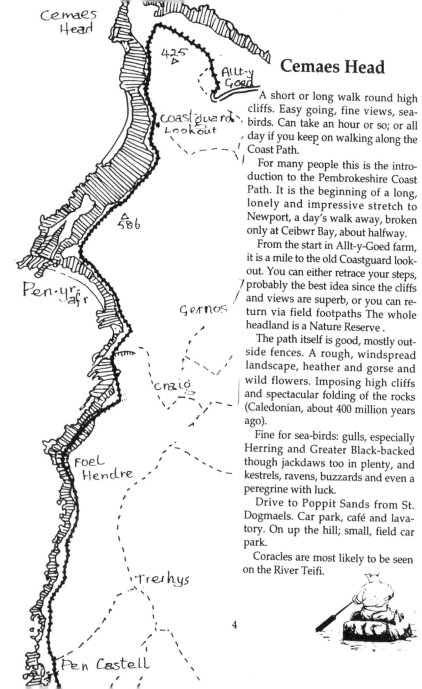

Cemaes Head

A short or long walk round high cliffs. Easy going, fine views, sea-birds. Can take an hour or so; or all day if you keep on walking along the Coast Path.

For many people this is the introduction to the Pembrokeshire Coast Path. It is the beginning of a long, lonely and impressive stretch to Newport, a day's walk away, broken only at Ceibwr Bay, about halfway.

From the start in Allt-y-Goed farm, it is a mile to the old Coastguard lookout. You can either retrace your steps, probably the best idea since the cliffs and views are superb, or you can return via field footpaths The whole headland is a Nature Reserve .

The path itself is good, mostly outside fences. A rough, windspread landscape, heather and gorse and wild flowers. Imposing high cliffs and spectacular folding of the rocks (Caledonian, about 400 million years ago).

Fine for sea-birds: gulls, especially Herring and Greater Black-backed though jackdaws too in plenty, and kestrels, ravens, buzzards and even a peregrine with luck.

Drive to Poppit Sands from St. Dogmaels. Car park, café and lavatory. On up the hill; small, field car park.

Coracles are most likely to be seen on the River Teifi.

4

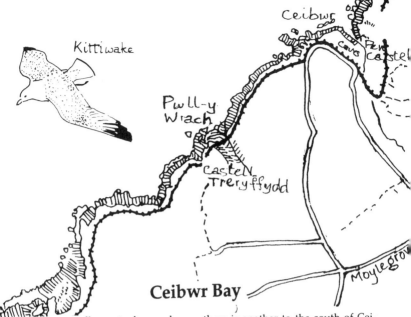

Kittiwake

Pwll-y-Wrach

Castell Treryffydd

Ceibwr

Cave

Pen castell

Moylegrove

Ceibwr Bay

A short walk centred round a lovely little bay bequeathed to the National Trust by Wynford Vaughan-Thomas. Good roadside parking, good walking on the Coast Path both north and south.

This is a place well worth going to for itself, for a picnic or for the scenery. For walking it is better to go for a mile or so along the Coast Path and retrace one's steps than to try a round walk.

For a long walk, this is something like halfway between Cemaes Head and Newport, two hours or so from one and about three from the other. But note that there are no exits from the Path between here and Newport and the going is hard.

To the north of Ceibwr, up the field, and in front of the house on to the Coast Path. Pencastell is the site of an Iron Age promontory fort; and

there is another to the south of Ceibwr past Pwll y Wrach, The Witch's Cauldron.

Marginally, it is more attractive walking to this spectacularly collapsed cave than going north, but though the path is good, be careful with small children since the grass slopes to sheer cliffs.

Ceibwr is splendid for seals, September and October especially; and very good for sea-birds: gulls of all kinds, shags, cormorants and also for the rare chough – a red-beaked, red-legged crow. And the faulting in the rock is as imposing as at Cemaes Head. No facilities of any kind.

Up the valley from Ceibwr is the village of Moylgrove, named after the wife of Robert Martin, first Norman Lord of Cemaes. Ceibwr was once a port.

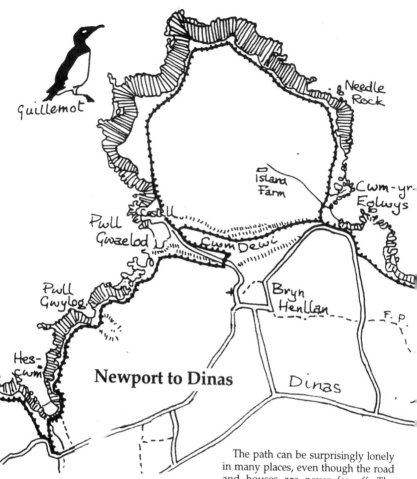

Guillemot

Needle Rock

Island Farm

Cwm-yr-Eglwys

Pwll Gwaelod

Castell

Cwm Dewi

Pwll Gwylog

Bryn Henllan

F.P.

Hes-cwm

Newport to Dinas

Dinas

A very fine stretch of coast, either as one long walk, or several short ones. The path is good and the walking easy. This is good, pleasant walking for the whole family, with attractive beaches for a picnic, though Cwm yr Eglwys and Pwllgwaelod can get crowded in summer. Aberrhigian, Aberfforest and Hescwm never are.

The path can be surprisingly lonely in many places, even though the road and houses are never far off. The cliffs are from 100 to 200 ft. but sheer and dangerous for the unwary; and at Dinas Head they rise majestically to nearly 500ft. You could omit Dinas Island if you are walking along the coast, but it would be a pity, because it is so fine and not too arduous even for the very young or the elderly if taken easily. It is now owned by the National Trust.

The wild flowers are splendid indeed: celandines and primroses, the blue squills, sea campion and the thick sweet scent of the gorse, even before the summer begins.

Sea-birds are fine anywhere, but especially round Dinas island: Herring, Greater and Lesser Black-backed gulls, razorbills, some guillemots, fulmars, shags, cormorants, choughs, crows, ravens, jackdaws, stone-chats in the thickets; buzzard and kestrel.

Alternative Walks:
(1) Start at the Parrog, with good parking. 3 miles to Cwm yr Eglwys, 1½ hours , returning on the road or back by the same way.
(2) Park at Parrog, walk the lot or part and get picked en route.
(3) Park at Cwm yr Eglwys or Pwllgwaelod, which are beaches either side of Dinas Island. Then walk round Dinas Head, 1⅜ miles, 1 hour.

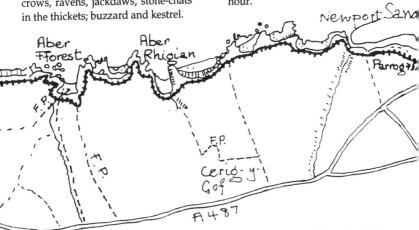

Cerrig y Gof, in a field by the A487 road near Aberrhigian is a celebrated group of collapsed Stone Age burial chambers. The ruined church at Cwm yr Eglwys was destroyed in a great gale in 1859; dedicated to St. Brynach, a 5th century saint with a strong local association in north Pembrokeshire.

Amenities at Parrog and pub and cafe at Pwllgwaelod.

(4) Park at Pwllgwaelod and walk to Hescwm, 1¼ miles, ¾ hour. Back the same way or on the narrow country road.
(5) For intermediate stretches: park on verge of A487 and take footpaths to Aberrhigian or Aberfforest. There's only room for a couple of cars, so get there early.
(6) A path through Cwm Dewi has been concreted making it, very unusually for a rural path, suitable for wheelchair users.

7

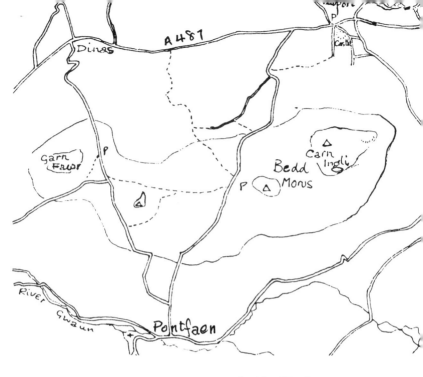

Carn Ingli and the Gwaun Valley

Short or long walks in lovely, unspoilt country; not to be missed.

Several approaches, easiest being from Dinas, signposted Cwm Gwaun. Park off the road on top and just walk. You can go either west over top Garn Fawr, unfenced land, among the mountain ponies. Or east, through the gate along the unmarked footpath. After 1½ miles you come to the Newport-Pontfaen road at Bedd Morus, Bronze Age standing stone.

If you come from the Fishguard direction either via Llanychaer or the narrow road from near the Morning Star on A487, you'll have passed the Holy Well at Llanllawer where you turn on to the hills by the church. Then you pass the Parc y Meirw (Field of the Dead), a celebrated line of huge stones in the hedge, believed from the Stone Age, but meaning unknown, or is it a calendrical alignment?

8

Coming from Newport where you turn at the sign Cwm Gwaun, you park at Bedd Morus and walk towards Carn Ingli. You won't see it at first but you'll reach it well inside an hour.

Any paths will be sheep tracks; it's best to keep over to the right where there is a fence marking the top fields in the Gwaun Valley farms. (If it's misty and you haven't a compass you can wander round in circles.) Go back the same way; but if you are being dropped and want a longer walk, a mile past Carn Ingli will bring you to a road leading back to Newport.

The walking is superb, the views as fine as you will see anywhere. Views both of the sea-coast, Ireland possibly, Snowdonia away to the north. Mountain views over to the Presely Hills, about four miles away as the crow flies, a splendid panoramic backdrop. It is not very high here, up to about 1,000 ft., 300 metres if you prefer, but the isolation is intense and after walking along the coast path, this seems like the top of the world.

There will be few people; for company you'll have sheep, wild mountain ponies; a pair of ravens, curlew, buzzard, larks and pipits perhaps, and maybe a fox. It is not a place to hurry; and the tussocks can be awkward too. It is fine at any time of the year though the colour of the heather, bracken and gorse makes it outstanding in the late summer and autumn. And in the snow, it is possibly better.

On Carn Ingli, 1,138 ft. high, is one of the best preserved prehistoric Iron Age camps in Britain. Natural rock outcrops are used and joined by an immense wall, never very high, probably never over 6 ft. high. And it was about 6 ft. thick too. There are numerous enclosures and hut circles.

It was up on Carn Ingli that the St. Brynach, to whom a number of churches in north Pembrokeshire are dedicated, is said to have communed with angels.

Incidentally, keep dogs under strict control in any area like this which is unfenced and where sheep are roaming free.

The Gwaun Valley presents a little difficulty; the footpaths are not too good. Many are not maintained because they were originally between farm and cottage or church. Sometimes they just seem to peter out.

You will have to do some walking on the road to get the feel of the country and it is hard to do round walks. There's a car park and picnic site at Cilrhedyn Bridge (between Pontfaen and Llanychaer).

Footpaths through land leased by the National Park; best to start at Pontfaen. Cross the river, go up the hill towards the church. Footpaths on the left, going parallel to the road and then on to Tregynon – 1½ miles

On the other side of the valley, good walking from Sychpant car park, up northwards.

The valley is quiet and steep-sided with woods of scrub oak, the river at the bottom, small farms with a good deal of rough land. The river rises to the north at Foel Eryr in the Preselies and reaches the sea at Lower Town in Fishguard. There is no road along the river till Llanychaer.

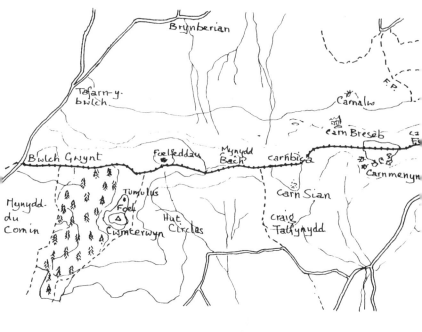

Preseli Hills

The walk across the top, described here, is only about 8 miles – an easy four hours, with lunch in the shelter of an outcrop. It is quite easy walking, with the advantage over the Coast Path of your being able to walk in line abreast and not in single file.

The views are superb, everything is clear, still, quiet and unspoilt. But watch out for boggy patches, especially lower down; and never come on a misty day. You need good boots too.

A trackway, believed to be from the Bronze Age, runs across, not quite the top, but a convenient contour. It ended at St. David's, terminus of a trade with Ireland.

The traditions of these early people are enshrined in the place-names and curious folk tales, especially that connected with king Arthur and the mysterious boar, Twrch Trwyth, who fought a desperate battle on Preseli. In the old legends of the Mabinogion, Preseli was a place of mystery.

Foel Cwmcerwyn (Preseli Top) is, at 1,760 ft., the highest point and it is afforested, apart from a tonsure. The historian Fenton noted that, 190 years ago, it was covered with the finest sward to the top unlike the "heath and stunted furze" of the other hills.

Now for the route. Incidentally, it isn't a "ridge" walk, but a broad undulating expanse, many high points being frequently obscured.

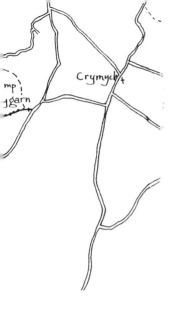

Park at Bwlch Gwynt and walk up with the Forestry plantation on the right. The conifer clad Foel Cwmcerwyn is over on the right. There were four Bronze Age burial cairns on top, Fenton excavated them in 1806; it was quite a circus with a long gaily dressed procession of ladies and gentlemen winding their way up Preseli for a picnic with their luncheon cart. But weather turned cold and threatening, so they all went quickly down to the inn at Maenclochog, still watched by the peasantry from miles around.

The hills themselves are geologically old, Ordovician rocks 400 to 500 million years old, shales and mudstones with igneous rocks forced up by volcanic action. These tumbled, jagged crags are of intrusive dolorite. It is the spotted version of this dolorite,

coming from here alone in Britain, that was identified 50 years ago with the rocks of the inner circle of Stonehenge. The later Ice Ages came up to about 1,000 ft. and when they retreated from the lower slopes, the stony "boulder clay" was left, a water-holding surface often producing a bog.

After 1½ mile the track is crossed by a theoretical public right of way going north towards Tafarn y Bwlch and south to Rosebush. There are hut circles ½ mile down to the left.

You leave Foel Feddau (Hill Sepulchres) a furlong to your left after a couple of miles. Down to your right is the great bowl of Cwm Cerwyn.

Not far from the road at Brynberian, 1½ miles north below Foel Feddau is Bedd yr Afanc (the Monster's Grave), a Neolithic burial chamber, dating back some 4,500 years.

Mynydd Bach is passed on the left after another ¾ mile.

Another right of way comes up ¼ mile further to the right. The Stones of the Sons of Arthur (Cerrig Meibion Arthur) are ¾ mile down on the same side. A car can be left down here on the road 1 mile below, if you want to start (or finish) halfway.

A mile past Mynydd Bach, the track goes to the north-east and you leave Carn Bica to the left with the ridge of Carn Goedog out beyond. Just to the right of the path, unfortunately off the sketch-map, is Bedd Arthur (Arthur's Grave), an oval shape of a dozen stones, never excavated. And ¼ mile further to the right is Carn Arthur.

Soon you pass Carn Breseb, ¼ mile to the left; beyond it, Carn Alw. Now, ½ mile more to Carn Meini, the main centre of the Blue stones. The track

goes to the north of it, but since there is no path to follow on the ground, go on down and explore the fantastic shapes of the ragged rocks.

Foel Drygarn, always darker than the others, looms over on the left. There is a further Bronze Age burial mound at Garn Ferched just on the left.

The track goes ¼ mile south of Foel Drygarn, but it is well worth deviating to explore the embankment and hut circles, possibly surprising, as we did once, a handsome fox. It is easy to strike down south east at Croesfihangel, where there was a Bronze Age burial mound dating back to about 1,000 B.C. with five burial urns in it.

If you want a more detailed map, you'll have to get the O.S. SN03 and SN13. The O.S. 145 is hardly good enough.

The "road" you have walked has had various names: Fleming's Way, Robber's Way, Roman Road, The Old Road (Yr Hen Ffordd), Pilgrims' Way. Some waymarking of a simple type would not be amiss.

Short Walks

You can make short walks from either end, retracing your steps. Round Foel Drygarn especially makes a good walk from the eastern end.

You can ascend the Preselies from either south or north sides. Most people prefer the former, and there is public right of way below Craig Talfynydd half way along. And at the Rosebush end, there are two good ways, one through the village and the other from the B4313 up to Cwmcerwyn.

On the north side, take one of the little side roads running from the Crosswell-Crymych road (not shown on the sketch map). The little roads peter out at the moor: a very good and uncrowded way to find a good parking place and uncrowded rough walking; some boggy patches. Don't be deterred. This little known approach is the best way for short walks in the Preselies, especially up to Carn Alw.

12

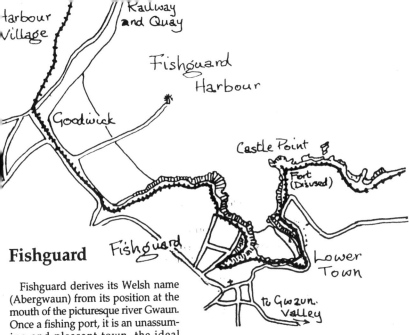

Fishguard

Fishguard derives its Welsh name (Abergwaun) from its position at the mouth of the picturesque river Gwaun. Once a fishing port, it is an unassuming and pleasant town, the ideal centre for the north of the county.

There are three parts: Lower Town, the oldest part; the main part up the hill; and a separate village, Goodwick, down the hill to the main harbour. Once a prospective terminus for trans-atlantic liners, it is now, as is Holyhead in the north, the port for the Irish ferry trade, tourists having replaced cattle.

You wouldn't come to Fishguard for any architectural masterpieces. There's a fine neo-classical chapel, Hermon, and a pleasant little Town Hall with a good Thursday market. A few Georgian houses have somehow escaped, mostly the houses are modern bungalows.

But surprisingly, since Fishguard was left out of the National Park, it is a jolly good place for walking. There is a good scenic Marine Walk, starting from the boat-yard by the bridge in Lower Town round to Goodwick. Depending on how fast you go, it's about one hours walk. Or, you can leave it at the Slade and go up in to the middle of the town. Fine views.

Or, shorter: from the Square, towards Lower Town; instead of going down the hill, go straight along Tower Hill (a dead end) for twenty minutes, above the Gwaun valley. Back the same way or struggle down a steep footpaths to the Gwaun Valley and back to Lower Town.

If you're energetic you can go past Goodwick up on to the rugged Pencaer Peninsula, part of which is dealt with on the next walk.

Strumble Head

Light House
Ynys
Meicel

Ynys Onen

Pen
Brush

Treathro

Porth Maen
Melyn

Tal-y-gaen
YHA

Garn
Fawr
Camp

Dinas
Mawr

Piollderi

Tref-Asser

Penbwchdy

14

Strumble Head to Pwllderi

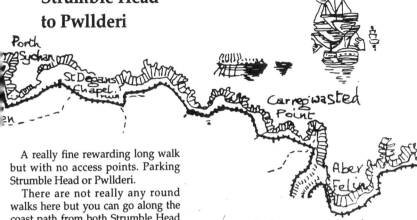

Porth Sychan
St Degans Chapel ruin
Carreg wasted Point
Aber Felin

A really fine rewarding long walk but with no access points. Parking Strumble Head or Pwllderi.

There are not really any round walks here but you can go along the coast path from both Strumble Head and Pwllderi for a mile or so in any direction and back again. The scenery and views are superb, the sea-birds plentiful, seals entrancing at Pwllderi.

There are no beaches on this stretch, but if you go from Strumble Head eastwards for 20 minutes, or from Tresinwen farm 10 minutes, there is a splendid little bay, Porthsychan, quiet and undisturbed. This long walk is one of the most attractive in the whole county: remote and wild, a rocky waste of heather, bracken and coarse grass. In one or two places the path is not too well-defined, but you can't go far wrong.

Strumble Head lighthouse, built in 1908, is no longer manned but it is always an interesting place to visit. It is immaculately shining and spick and span.

At Pwllderi is a Youth Hostel, in one of the finest situations imaginable. There are superb views down the coast towards St. David's. On the road near by is a memorial to the Welsh poet Dewi Emrys.

Behind Pwllderi towers Garn Fawr, on top of which is one of the most imposing hill forts in the county. Considering its size, few hut circles.

Several lines of stone ramparts connect the rock outcrops and there is an earth rampart and ditch. Best approached from the small car park on the landward side, on the road to Strumble Head.

Half a mile to the west of garn Fawr on the coast is Dinas Mawr, a fine cliff fort, three precipitous sides to the sea and a narrow neck with two stone banks on the landward side.

In the yard of the farm Tal-y-Gaer opposite the Youth Hostel is a very early circular corbelled hut, possibly an early monk's cell.

South of Pwllderi is Trefasser, said to be the birth-place of Bishop Asser, friend and biographer of Alfred the Great.

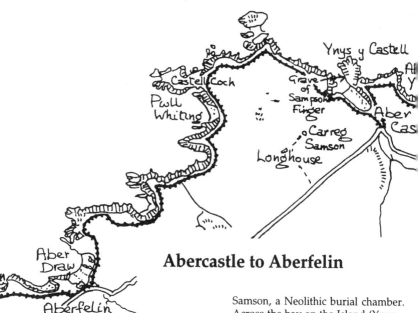

Abercastle to Aberfelin

A short walk on one of the most beautiful parts of the Coast Path. Parking both ends. The path is good, at times narrow. Go along the coast, from one bay to another, and back the same way, or by road via Trefin, which is shorter, but very pleasant. Abercastle was once a good little port in Elizabethan times exporting grain and butter, now a sailing harbour only; many houses are holiday cottages. No facilities except telephone.

Walk west along Coast Path past the fine lime kiln. Up to the left is Cwm Badau (Valley of the Boats); footpath up to the famous Carreg Samson, a Neolithic burial chamber. Across the bay on the Island (Ynys y Castell) is a presumed Iron Age hill fort and a mound named Grave of Samson's Finger, but no-one knows the origin of the names. For a very short walk go up the footpath past the burial chamber to Longhouse farmyard and back down the road.

Just under a mile is a fine Iron Age promontory fort on the end of a headland, Castell Coch, with two embankments and ditches, and about three acres enclosed inside. Fine beaches below, but inaccessible. The farm here is a well-known one, Longhouse, once a grange of the Bishop of St. David's when he had a palace in Trefin.

Aberfelin has a ruined mill by the shore, subject of a famous Welsh poem.

Lavatories at Abercastle, no refreshments either end but both in Trefin on the road back.

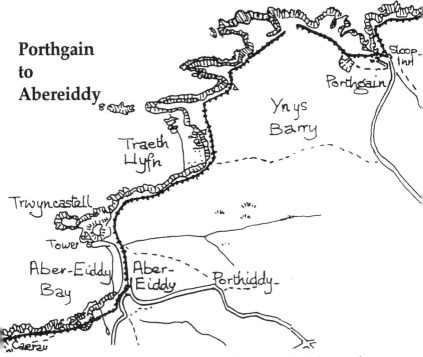

Porthgain to Abereiddy

Porthgain

Sloop Inn

Ynys Barry

Traeth Llyfn

Trwyncastell

Tower

Aber-Eiddy Bay

Aber-Eiddy

Porthiddy

Caerau

Short walk; 1½ miles with perhaps finest coastal scenery in the county. Path good, a little rutted by cattle in part. Return the same way. Good parking both ends.

The buildings to the west of the harbour are the remains of a stone crushing industry – the bins and crushing plant. Sailing ships and steamers came into the little harbour in Victorian and Edwardian times and took the roadstone as far as London and often to Bristol and north Devon ports. Bricks and slates were exported too. The plant was closed in 1931. The quarry itself can be reached in a few minutes along the cliff top, where the remains of quarry buildings can still be seen. Just under a mile brings you to a very fine beach,

Traethllwyn, reached down a long flight of steps.

Further on, the path branches: either go inland a little or stay on the cliff and, if you do, go and see the Blue Lagoon, a former slate quarry. Entrance was blasted away by fishermen, making a small fine harbour. The very blue water is extremely deep. Not for bathing.

Abereiddy was a quarry village. Buildings ruined now, but the National Trust who owns this stretch of coastline has an ongoing plan to preserve them. The place is famous for the tuning-fork graptolite fossils found in the slates on the beach.

No refreshments at Abereiddy, but lavatory. Pub, restaurant, lavatory at Porthgain.

St. David's Head

Short walks around famous rocky headland and cliffs. Nearly a mile to the Headland, another 1½ miles or so round and back, either same way or by footpath via farm.

Easy walking; wonderful views; much of interest historically; beaches and amenities; all adds up to one of the best walks anywhere; quite a lot of other people think so too, in summer. It's a place for wandering.

Cross over from the car park and you pass where St. Patrick's Chapel was; early seamen's and pilgrims' chapel. Legend say St. Patrick, maybe a Pembrokeshire man, had his vision of converting the Irish here.

Farmhouse inland, Ty Gwyn (White House), is supposedly the site where

St. David was educated.

There is a Neolithic burial chamber a little way inland from the headland, and two more smaller ones up near where the First World War Hydrophone station was on Carn Llidi.

Right on the headland (167ft. high) is an Iron Age promontory fort with 8 hut circles inside and a huge defensive stone wall, the Warrior's Dyke.

If you stand looking seawards up by Carn Llidi and the bracken is not too high, you can see the outlines of early Celtic field patterns.

Common land, now National Trust owned. They are trying to re-establish traditional practices such as grazing and bracken cutting to benefit wildlife.

18

St. David's Peninsula

Long walks from Whitesand round to Solva. About 13 miles altogether (4½ hours), but can be made into shorter stretches.

Shorter walks: Whitesand to St. Justinian's: 2½ miles, ¾ hour. St. Justinian's to Porth Clais: 4 miles, 1¾ Porth Clais to Caerfai: 2 miles, ¾ hour. Caerfai to Solva: 4¼ miles, 2 hours. Car parking at all the above, sometimes busy in summer. Footpath access at: Porthsele; from Lower Treginnis; St. Non's: the Chapel, not the Hotel Caerbwdi (car park not far); Trelerw; Llandruidion via Ffos y Mynach; Mutton Farm to Porth y Rhaw, Llanunwas. So you can shorten the walks by using any of above (the last 3 are not shown on our map).

From Lower Treginnis round to Solva the cliffland is mostly owned and traditionally managed by the National Trust.

Round St. David's Peninsula is as fine a coastal walk as you are ever likely to find. If you do it all in one, you'll have to be met the other end or get two cars. The path is good everywhere and it is easy going.

The flat, windswept peninsula, with its rocky outcrops, clustered farms and sparse trees, has a curious fascination.

The city is no more than a village in size. It lies at the centre and roads radiate to the coast, which is rocky, with low but sheer cliffs, and indented with small bays.

First bay south of Whitesand is Porthsele, and at very low water it adjoins. The Path follows the cliff closely. Outside the farm fences, there is, for the most part, a good grassy path with heather, gorse and bracken around.

Sea-birds, to be seen everywhere, and seals, most frequently in the autumn.

Off the coast lies Ramsey Island, 600 acres, 2 miles long and 1 mile wide. Boat trips in summer; famous for birds and seals.

A little to the south is Castell Heinif, an early Iron Age promontory fort with two banks.

Round to Porthlysgi, a splendid 2 mile stretch. Lysgi was an early Irish raider. He landed, and killed Boia, a local Celtic chieftain who lived at Clegyr Foia, one mile inland – a mass of igneous rock not eroded by the sea like the flattish landscape around. On the rock is a quite substantial Iron Age hill fort and underneath it was found a New Stone Age dwelling.

Round the headland is Porth Clais, once the port for St. David's. It is at the mouth of the River Alun, 1 mile from the city. St. David was baptised here.

As early as 1358, cargoes were brought in for the cathedral. In Elizabethan times, timber came from Ireland and corn, malt and wool went to Bristol and Barnstaple.

The harbour wall has long been ruined and although coal was being brought here even after the war for the gas works (now a car park), there wasn't much of a port after 1800. Small boats use the harbour now.

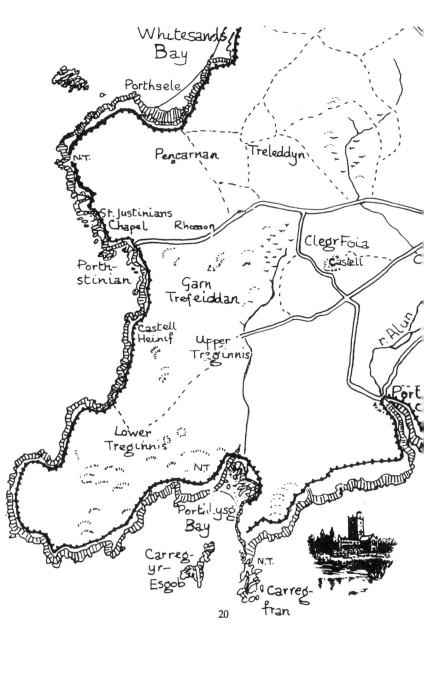

Whitesands Bay

Porthsele

N.T.

Pencarnan

Treleddyn

St. Justinians
Chapel

Rhosson

ClegrFoia

Castell

Porth-
stinian

Garn
Trefeiddan

Castell
Heinif

Upper
Tregunnis

r. Alun

Port

Lower
Tregunnis

N.T.

Port Clyso
Bay

N.T.

Carreg-
yr-
Esgob

Carreg-
fran

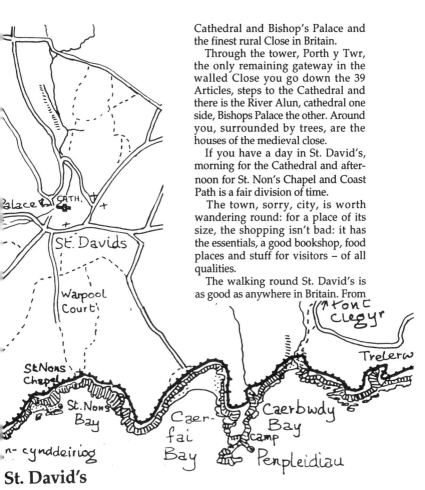

Cathedral and Bishop's Palace and the finest rural Close in Britain.

Through the tower, Porth y Twr, the only remaining gateway in the walled Close you go down the 39 Articles, steps to the Cathedral and there is the River Alun, cathedral one side, Bishops Palace the other. Around you, surrounded by trees, are the houses of the medieval close.

If you have a day in St. David's, morning for the Cathedral and afternoon for St. Non's Chapel and Coast Path is a fair division of time.

The town, sorry, city, is worth wandering round: for a place of its size, the shopping isn't bad: it has the essentials, a good bookshop, food places and stuff for visitors – of all qualities.

The walking round St. David's is as good as anywhere in Britain. From

St. David's

One road approaches from Fishguard and the other from Haverfordwest, they meet in Cross Square, and you wonder where the Cathedral is: well, you can just see its tower rising from the Alun valley.

Like every other place in Pembrokeshire, St. David has few architectural pretensions; but it has its splendid

the centre of the city the driveway to Warpool Court Hotel leads also to St. Non's Chapel and Well; and then on to the Coast Path.

You can't descend at St. Non's Bay, but it's a short walk to Caerfai, a popular beach; and back on a rural road to St. David's. Car parking in the city and at Caerfai.

Newgale to Druidston Haven via Nolton Haven

Short walks along beaches and cliffs.

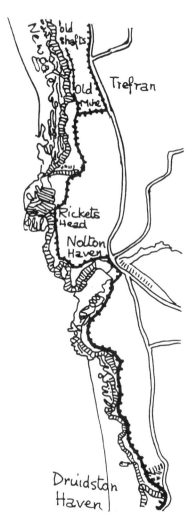

Newgale to Nolton Haven 1½ miles, ½ hour or so; Nolton Haven to Druidston Haven: 1 mile, ½ hour also. Interesting walk, most of it along the beach at low water, or on Coast Path; return by Coast Path or by coast road. Good parking at Newgale, and at Nolton; roadside parking at Druidston.

The north end of Newgale is the limit of the English half of the county. Also of the oldest rocks for here the geologically younger Coal Measures begin.

The beach, 1½ miles of it, has a huge natural storm bank of pebbles, due to sea action.

At the southern end was once a chapel. The legend is that St. Caradoc's body, being taken along the old Welsh road to St. David's for burial stayed miraculously dry when his bearers sheltered from a storm.

Start at Newgale and walk either along the beach at low water and scramble up the cliff; or take the road for a mile and turn back to the coast at the signpost. If you want to walk north, excellent cliff walking towards Solva.

South of Newgale is the site of Trefrane colliery, worked in Victorian times, until 1905. It went under the sea and the coal taken by traction engine to Nolton. From Nolton Haven, you go up past the Chapel to the Coast Path. Round the headland and at low water you can go down to the beach at Madoc's Haven. A fine long beach up to Druidston (from 12th century Norman Knight, nothing to do with Druids).

Cafe, shop, lavatory at Newgale. Inn at Nolton; hotel at Druidston.

Marloes Peninsula

The Marloes peninsula offers long and short walks with wonderful scenery and, especially, on Skomer and Skokholm, internationally renowned bird sanctuaries, though these need special access.

For a long walk, you can use the Coast Path; for short walks, divide up the path into sections; but the coast is more interesting than the interior. Whole peninsula is National Trust.

Two good car parks: one near Runwayskiln serving the beach, the other near Martin's Haven, serving the end of the peninsula the Deer Park and Skomer. (Trips to Skomer start from Martin's Haven.)

the map down to Renny Slip and west to east, walk along to Gateholm and Marloes Sands. A footpath leads via Runwayskiln and to the main road; walk back to Martin's Haven. Or if you use Runwayskiln Car Park, you can walk to the beach, then westwards to Renny Slip.

If you are historically minded, struggle up onto Gateholm (low water) which once had over a hundred huts; the circles are still there, suggesting either Iron Age or Monastic occupation, introducing a slice of history into the holiday atmosphere of the beach.

You go the whole length of the beach and take a footpath up to the village or you can take the path by Gateholm and up to Marloes Mere and Runwayskiln.

As well as being a wonderful beach, Marloes Sands is renowned geologically, see especially the Three Chimneys.

So, if you use the latter, you can walk round the Deer Park which is splendid; it was the largest Iron Age defended settlement in Pembrokeshire. Fine view over Skomer and Jack Sound.

Or you can walk anti-clockwise on

23

In the winter, there's a wealth of wildfowl. The wildlife has nothing exclusive to the area, but there might be ravens and choughs, oystercatchers, and the clicking of stone-chat in the gorse and brambles; grey wagtails too.

If you are interested in sea-birds, a visit to Skomer, which will last all day, is not to be missed.

West Angle Bay to Freshwater West

An outstanding walk with magnificent coastal scenery of Old Red Sandstone cliffs. This is a longish walk; 4 miles 2 hours walking time. Car parking good at both ends.

Park at West Angle Bay – close to the beach with good café close by.

Open cliff by the R.A.F. installation and down to East block house which is the ruin of an early Haven defence fort from Tudor times. Rat Island opposite.

On the mainland by Sheep Island is Skomer neck Camp, a fine Iron Age fort. A bank and ditch cuts off half an acre and a natural gully cuts off the rest of the promontory. Fenton, quoting the Elizabethan George Owen, says there was a tower here once, a retreat for the invading Normans.

Then after Parsons Quarry Bay and Guttle Hole, with Monk's Rock off-shore, there is another fort between West and East Pickard Bay.

Inland from here was the war-time Angle Airfield, and the B4320 runs half a mile inland. There are no inland footpaths to provide short cuts, and the interior – old Angle airfield – the less said about it the better.

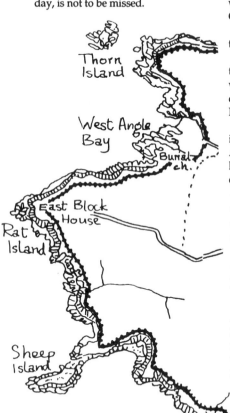

Thorn Island

West Angle Bay

Bunat ch.

East Block House

Rat Island

Sheep Island

West

Pickard Bay East

24

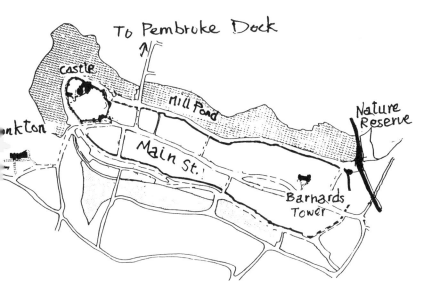

Pembroke – a medieval town

It may not seem like it on a fine summer's day, with visitors thronging the busy streets, but this is the model of a medieval town.

Behind looms the most imposing of all Norman castles, stronghold of earliest Marcher Lords, ruthless invaders of Wales and later Ireland. This castle may lack the aesthetic of Beaumaris and Conway, but it was never once taken by the Welsh.

From this impregnable fortress, the de Clares – Strongbow – and the formidable William Marshall invaded Ireland and held it for the English Kings. Eventually, Henry, the first Welsh monarch of Britain was born here.

It is privately owned and, ridiculously, omitted from most official literature. Most rewarding of all west Wales castles; don't miss it. Literature in the castle bookshop.

Now, a walk round the town. As you will see the southern half of the medieval walls are still there and the shape of the town is now as it was then. Two fine medieval churches, much restored, and some fine houses – Georgian mostly. Booklet by Chamber of Trade.

And in addition, its own Nature Reserve, the Upper Mill Pond. It is the eastern end of what was once a tidal creek extending from below the castle. Fine range of water birds. Good beaches at West Angle and Broad Haven, near Bosherston.

Stack Rocks to Broad Haven

A fine walk, an unusual landscape for Pembrokeshire. This goes right from Stack Rocks to Broad Haven and the next two maps cover the area. This map goes past Bullslaughter Bay to Crickmail Down; and the next one onto St. Govans Head and then to Broad Haven.

This is, irritatingly for a National Park, subject to the arbitrariness of the Ministry of Defence. This is a wonderful landscape – superb limestone cliffs and grass sword and the desolation produced by the Army replaces some fine old farmhouses and an area where the Mirehouses and Cawdors effected an agricultural revolution.

Wave action caused the flatness, and the caves, blowholes, isolated stacks, arches and inlets so typical of limestone are due to erosion by sea, rain and streams.

you count them) dark and damp, an empty bellcote, a stone altar at the east end, a single slit above. There is a well below the chapel, protected by a stone hood. It was famous for healing though it is dry now. Nobody knows who St. Govan was: the Arthurian Gawaine of the Round Table; or Goven, wife of a Celtic King or Gobham, Irish contemporary of St. David.

The path, being on Ministry of Defence land, may be closed between Stack Rocks and Broad Haven. Firing notices in local papers. Usually open weekends.

Bosherston and Broad Haven are popular in the summer. The village is fine for tea at the cafe and a walk round the lily ponds.

Previously an inlet of the sea the ponds are a part of the lakes created artificially at the end of the 17th century. This was part of the Stackpole Estate, now National Trust.

There is a lovely white carpet of water lilies in the early summer.

This is the best, almost the only, coarse fishing in the county; and as well as the roach, perch, tench, pike there is a good bird population. Her-

Wonderful sea-birds to be seen at Stack Rocks; wild flowers on the cliffs, Iron Age forts at Flimston, Crocksydam, and Buckspool. Lots of these cliffs have become very popular with climbers. Car park.

And St. Govan's: see the chapel. Small, rough, stone cell, from 13th century; down 52 rough stone steps (supposed to be different each time

ons, moorhens, swans, coots, mallards, even kingfishers may be seen.

And there is an impressive Iron Age fort; the steep slopes have ditches and ramparts added to make more effective defence.

26

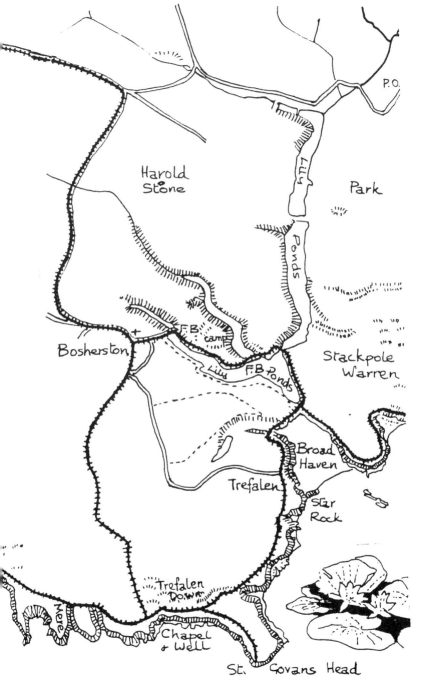

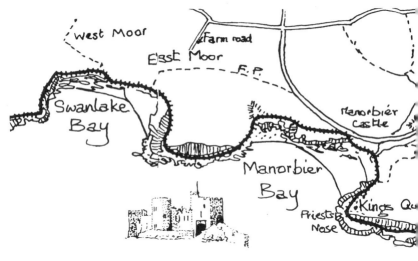

Manorbier to Swanlake Bay

Short walk along the Coast Path: 2½ miles, 1 hour or under. You can walk back along the cliffs the same way or via the footpath from East Moor Farm. Freshwater East is a further 2 miles along the coast, 1 hour.

Car park at Manorbier, and at Freshwater East. Refreshments at latter, toilets at both. Nothing at Swanlake.

This can be a pleasant afternoon's walk. Swanlake is never too crowded since there is no car access, only footpaths from East and West Moor farms.

Peaceful landscape and a coast of Old Red Sandstone rocks with up-ended strata, cracks and fissures, so be careful. Manorbier is a picture-book setting for the castle and church. Don't miss seeing the castle. There are rarely any so well-preserved; it was never "reduced". It is of 12th and 13th century construction. There is a fine gateway tower, and a huge round tower; inside, a Great Hall and vaulted chapel. Other original inter-

ior domestic buildings have disappeared in favour of newer ones.

Giraldus Cambrensis (the Welshman) was born here in 1146, Norman on his father's side, Welsh on his mother's. A remarkably able Churchman and protagonist of the Celtic Church against Canterbury, he struggled most of his life to become Bishop of St. David's but Canterbury and the King were too much for him.

To Giraldus, Manorbier was the "Paradise of all Wales"; there were nut-groves, orchards and vineyards and fishponds in the valley below the castle and church, where is now a sandy scrub.

The church too is old, 12th century, at least the nave. Bits were added: chancel, transepts and battlemented tower so typical of South Pembrokeshire churches.

To the east of the beach, pleasant walking on the cliffs; there is a Neolithic burial chamber.

Tenby to Saundersfoot

Fine walk along the Coast path. Tenby to Monkstone 2¼ miles, 1 hour. Monkstone to Saundersfoot: 1 mile, ½ hour. There is a public road down to Trevayne Farm and a path to Monkstone from the farm, but it is not a public right of way; courtesy of the farmer only. But it is possible to make two walks. Car parking can be difficult in summer pretty well anywhere round here.

The start is up on North Cliff, Tenby, on the old Waterwynch Lane, a pleasant shady bridleway off the coast but rural enough for you to meet a fox.

At the top of the hill on the seaward side is a stile giving access to Allen's view, a wonderful spot.

The Coast Path skirts Waterwynch (though the beach is down on the right) and the path leads to the coast, where it stays up to Monkstone. It can be muddy round Waterwynch in wet weather.

The Coast Path is not too well marked at a couple of places at times, and there are a couple of surprisingly strenuous stretches, but in general it is fine for all walkers, except the elderly, who would be advised not to go far beyond Waterwynch.

Public footpath at Swallowtree, halfway from Monkstone to Saundersfoot. One of the most wooded sections of the Coast Path. End on the beach if low water or skirt inland.

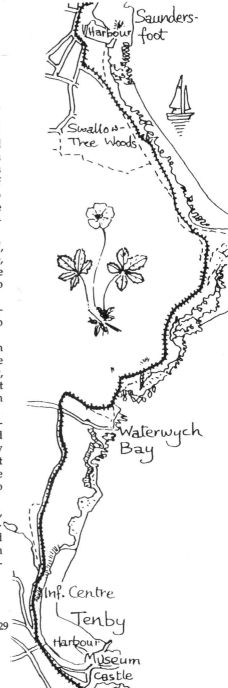

The Knights' Way – Woodland Walks

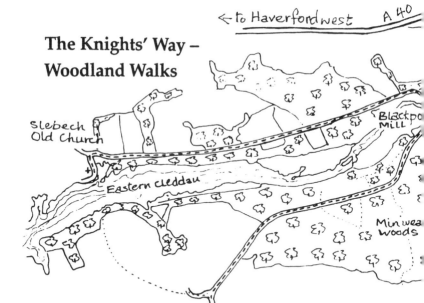

Here are some fine woodland walks, in the centre of the county. The Knights in question are the Templars and Hospitallers, rather more concerned with Palestine than Pembrokeshire. The "Way" links places which the Knights were connected with; a little tenuous perhaps but a good idea.

It links the wooded centre of the county – which we've chosen here – with the south-east, through Templeton, Ludchurch and Amroth. There's a County Council Leaflet about it.

Here we are suggesting a good Forestry Commission Slebech walk starting from the car park a little past Blackpool Mill by the roadside. There is a descriptive leaflet and little markers along the way.

Secondly the walk from Blackpool Mill on a footpath over the bridge in to Slebech. This has been labelled as the Daucleddau Trail, or a little part of it. It is beside the River Cleddau for a mile or so to the old Hospitallers' ruined church – return the same way. Car Park at Blackpool Mill which is itself interesting and has toilets, café and shop.

Thirdly, south-east, or perhaps more properly east by south, through Canastan Woods, which are themselves filled with footpaths.

Like Pencelli Forest these are part of an ancient forest: it was ancient even in medieval times and probably was pre-historic, anomalous in what is now the least forested county in Wales.

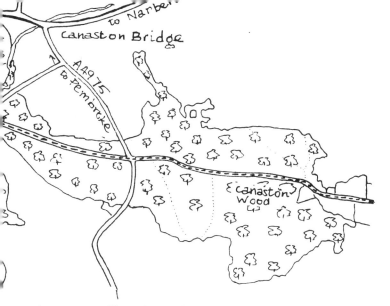

Other Woodland Walking

Haroldston Wood at Broad Haven near Haverfordwest, National Park managed. important for wildlife, but you'll be lucky to see much. Very pleasant walking: return possibly by Coast Path. Start at footpath at Broad Haven Car park.

Upton Castle Woodland quite different. Privately planted at Upton Castle, now managed by National Park. Good walk, many species. Signposted at A477 at Cosherston near Pembroke.

Pengelli was forest, ancient even in early Tudor times. At Pont Baldwin at the A487 just past Velindre Farchog, turn left. Lovely minor road to Cardigan, past Iron Age Castell Henllys on your right, over a ford and Pengelli is on your right. Nature Reserve, always uncrowded. Keep to footpaths.

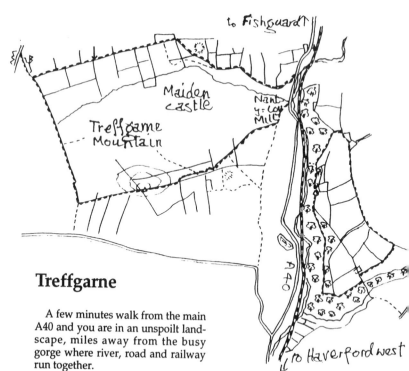

Treffgarne

A few minutes walk from the main A40 and you are in an unspoilt landscape, miles away from the busy gorge where river, road and railway run together.

Attractive walk on footpaths on rough – but not *too* rough – country: that's the left-hand dotted rectangle in the map. Hut circles, an ancient fort and wonderful panoramas

On the right of the main road is a woodland and field walk. No parking here – you park ¼ mile back in a large lay-by, which is also for the first walk. Signposted.

A third, possibly better walk is actually at Nant-y-Coy Mill, splendid water-wheel at the back. Mr Wilson at the Mill, has done his own leaflet in a little more detail than the County Council have.

Plumstone

There is a similar type of walk to Trefgarn a bit further west – mid county high, rough common land at Plumstone mountain. The County Council has signposted it. This, like Treffgarne, is high if rough land, of ancient volcanic rock, which is the divide between Welsh and English speakers: perhaps the Normans thought this land not worth appropriating.

Access easy: off B4300 Haverfordwest – Croesgoch road. Limited roadside parking.